THE GREAT SPIDER TREK

HADRIAN'S WALL
IN EIGHT LEGS

DORIS HANCOCK
AND FRIENDS

First Published in 2014 by
Songster Publications
Little Neston
Wirral

British Library Cataloguing in Publication Data.
A catalogue record of this book is available from the British Library.

ISBN 9780956307170

Available from
Birkenhead Press Ltd,
14 Appin Road,
Birkenhead,
Merseyside,
CH41 9HH

Printed in Great Britain by Birkenhead Press Ltd.

THE GREAT SPIDER TREK

Acknowledgements and thanks to:

Cath Stevenson for major planning
Alison McCandlish for contacting Centrepoint
All eight map readers for each leg
Tim Hancock for press contacts and photos
Tim Brown for accounting and "send off"
Ambleside Rotary Club
Alan Gaunt for publishing
Norman McCandlish for songs and ditties
Margaret Burford for deciphering written accounts
ALL ENCOURAGERS

Without any of these it would not have happened.

Hadrian's Spider Trek (how it came to be)

One day I walked into a shop, saw a greatly reduced book - *Hadrian's Wall Path* - I bought it. It reminded me of a display I saw in Tullie House (Carlisle Museum) on Hadrian's Wall, in retirement. I was very impressed by it, it became a "must Do" (just a visit) but it never happened.

I took the book home and read it from cover to cover- it had absolutely every bit of information you could wish for - maps, distances, what to wear, where to stay, history of each area, what specially to look for, flowers, birds, people, methods of building, weather possibilities, what not to do, what to drink and carry. It had complete large scale maps with notes like – wonderful views, keep on the other side of the hedge, uneven steps, avoid walking in line etc. Every stile and kissing gate was noted. Total distance 84 miles approximately. (a lot less than I would have thought.)

I guessed I could walk five miles a day - so we could walk five miles, stay the night, walk another five miles and go home. Do this eight times, once a month - March to October JOB DONE

Next, I must tell someone - so I told Cath - she said she thought it was a great idea and thought many people would want to join in - this proved to be true. Everyone we told was enthusiastic and likewise thought it was a "great idea." Not one person said, "Don't be stupid at your age" (95). I still find that difficult to believe - but it's true!

So Hadrian's Spider Trek was my logo, as a spider has eight legs - each visit would be one leg and we would gather together at the centre of the web to eat and chat in the evening.

Cath drew up a plan and the logo - each leg had a group to organise our trip: dogs, transport, food etc. Alison contacted

Centrepoint for balloons, tee shirts etc. and media. Tim Hancock set up a website. Tim Brown dealt with paying in cash.

It became obvious that this was an opportunity to help a deserving cause - so we walked for *Centrepoint* which deals with every aspect of rescuing young people from the streets (sleeping rough). They are given a room of their own in purpose built premises with skilled and devoted staff dealing with personal troubles, then delivering them from homelessness through to regaining self-respect, onto training for suitable types of employment, making friends and becoming an equal or even better than some of us folk. Tim Brown told me the then total was £8,881-50 - phew!

So what you have here are notes written at the time by myself and the friends in each leg - a reminder of things as they are.

Doris Hancock.

Introduction by Cath Stevenson

I am hoping that this journal will build up over the next seven months to become a fascinating account of the Spider Trek. Whilst the rest of the world maybe celebrating the Queen's Diamond Jubilee and the 2012 Olympic Games, our family and friends will be celebrating the amazing life of one woman, our Doris.

My Mum used the word 'funniosity' a lot when we were little. It was usually used affectionately to describe someone who looked or behaved a bit differently, or said funny things and she used it to describe me and my brother and sister when as children we did daft things.

For me Doris is a funniosity and I know my Mum would agree – they were best friends. Doris is always giggling about daft things and daft people. This makes her great fun to be with. She and I have always had the ability to look at something, catch each other's eye, then burst out laughing. She and Mum were always doing it – it must have driven my Dad mad! And we all know that Doris' laugh is quite unique and memorable!

So let's keep a very personal record of this fantastic Hadrian's Wall Walk, so that at the end of it, we have a book that Doris will treasure forever. Let's have some of Doris's pearlers and quotes from conversations that other walking companions may like to read. Some little pencil sketches if you are the artistic type, or even if you are not... Lots of observations of the Wall Path and its surrounds, maybe of people you meet on the way...
Pen a poem about the Wall, the nature, the pouring rain...

Cath Stevenson.

Cath & Geoff Stevenson (Huddersfield, West Yorkshire)
My Mum was her best friend in St Annes. Doris like an Auntie to me, Alison and Hugh. She has known me since I was 18 mths old (60 years!) when we all lived in St Annes in the Congregational Church Manse, my dad being the Minister.

Tim Brown (Ambleside and Newcastle)
Neighbour and good friend to Doris at Belle Vue Lane Ambleside.

Nick and Lorraine Hancock and Michelle
Nick is Doris's Nephew, Lorraine is his wife and Michelle is their daughter

Mike and Gwyn Arnott and Chris Arnott.
(Chris - St Annes; Mike and Gwyn- Lavenham nr Colchester)
Chris is my step-mother, she has known Doris from the 1950s. Mike is my step-brother and Gwyn is his wife. Doris has known Mike since he was a baby

Judith and Peter Landau (Ross on Wye, Herefordshire)
Judith is my cousin and Peter is her husband. Doris has known Judith she was a small child visiting her Auntie Jeanne and Uncle Doug (my parents) in Lytham St Annes.

Alison and Norman McCandlish
 (Ballinluig, nr Pitlochry, Perthshire)
Alison is my sister, Norman my brother-in-law. Doris has known Alison since she was a toddler.

Ian Sinclair and Richard Morte (Sheffield, S Yorkshire)
Ian has known Doris for a long time, since he and I were in college together at Bretton Hall. He is one of my best friends and Richard is his partner, also a good friend.

Tim and Jo Hancock (Ireby, nr Kirkby Lonsdale N Yorkshire.)
Tim is Doris's other nephew, Jo is his wife.

OTHER FRIENDS AND FAMILY WHO JOINED US
FOR THE LAST DAY'S WALK INTO BOWNESS
AND/OR THE PARTY AT WALLSEND GUEST HOUSE.

Barbara Crompton (Windermere) Friend of Doris from church

Richard and Kate Arnott (Edinburgh)
My step-brother and his wife. Doris has known Richard almost from birth. Richard was my best friend when we were children.

Hugh Stewart (Durham)
My brother. Doris has known him since he was a small child.

THE FIRST LEG

Hadrian's Wall Trek
Leg I Day 1 Wallsend to Tyne Bridge by Doris

Two days before we were due to leave I developed a very painful right leg and could hardly walk to the Parish Centre to see the AgeUK editor of their magazine. Only two days to go and I wondered if I would even start. At the Health Centre I had an emergency talk with the doctor who could find nothing amiss and I came home with some tablets and the thought that I might not be able to start.

Well, we did start, Cath and Geoff arrived on time so we donned our Centrepoint tee shirts and went out to a fine day. The journey was good and I was amazed at Cath's ability to find her way through a devious route to the house where we were to leave the car. We then took a taxi to Wallsend. The media were all there, having kept in contact with much phoning. There were three groups from radio and television and it seemed to take a very long time for them all to get set up. One of them sent me off to the toilet while they did all this. The man, who had phoned earlier asked me the same question three times: why was I doing it as he had heard, he said, that I wanted to do the walk before I died. I told him it was not true and I would not have used that word anyway – it was probably someone's idea of a joke. Tim Brown, my neighbour, brought along three of his friends to give me a good send off which they did – but not until noon.

I had enjoyed watching all the school children running about among an open area of Roman remains and finding things out at the Visitor Centre. I knew before very long that it was going to be a very painful trip and I slowed down before we had gone very far. Cath actually said "Don't worry we can always get a taxi back." I thought - more difficult today, then tomorrow IMPOSSIBLE but just kept going, knocking up each mile, imagining what it would feel like if I never reached the end.

I developed a habit of saying "not good" when asked how the leg was. Each time we stopped for a rest it was a little better on starting again but very soon reverted to the pain. I kept trying different ways of walking, kidding myself it was a bit better, but it always reverted. So that was the walking part, no-one complained about the showers so we endured the first day's walk.

Tim told us all about the history of commerce, the ship building, the coal industry, the architecture which I thought magnificent: beautiful buildings for the workers, which had been built to look good as well as being homes; intriguing designs for windows and arches, overhangs even roofs - I could go on forever. There were plaques, praising men who had created all these industries, monuments of all kinds – a real outdoor museum – quite a lot were formed from metal parts of machinery from the past.

All the way along the riverside was interesting, we met locals too, for example, two men lying on the boards, fishing lines in the water it didn't matter whether they caught any fish, they were enjoying relaxing in the sun and peacefulness. I asked them what they caught and then I couldn't understand the lingo when they told me. Along this riverside walk we saw seven bridges and I was thrilled to see the "Blinking Eye" operating just as we reached it. It is the newest bridge with a complete road, footpaths and rails raised by hundreds of pulleys.

We had had a third interview along the track as we ate our sandwiches, all very pleasant and informal. Towards the beginning we saw some ducks we could not name and later we saw an enormous collection of pigeon lofts and watched for quite a long time the release of a flock which flew round and round and round to get their bearings. We had to carry on before they finally got off. The trees which bloom before leaves were just beginning to burst open.

Our hotel overnight was a disappointment to say the least – only one pillow and No towels
> No soap
> No tea tray
> No tumbler
> No waste bin
> No hot water
> No en suite toilet
> No breakfast

BUT when we came in later in the evening after a meal out, the chap who had seen us on TV made us a cup of coffee and shared his chocolate bar with us.

HOWEVER everywhere was very clean and I had in my room an enormous wardrobe with five shelves, three drawers at the bedside and two under the bed. Newcastle was extremely busy, Friday rush hour. At the restaurant for our evening meal we had to move tables because of the noise, just over a low wall where they threw their empty bottles. By then the TV had been seen by many people and the young waiters collected £4 for our cause.

Day 2 Tyne Bridge to Tyneside River Country Park by Doris

We started off with breakfast at a riverside pub about 8.30 in lovely sunshine. Tim joined us again and we finally started off on our day's trek unrushed and still interesting. Cath had been out to the local park in the early morning and we had all managed a delightful hot bath. The various information boards and works of art, especially those formed from bits of machinery left behind by the now absent industries were behind us.

Near to a dock, rather like the Liverpool one, we had a morning coffee and when we finally came to the end of the river track Tim caught the bus back to his flat. The track led us up a hill and finally we were walking along a main road, the A695

We had met a group of people at Wallsend, who came and did a bit of the wall each year when the fit took them. We had to cross this very busy road. Cars hooted at us because of our shirts and balloons which they had seen on TV the night before and here again we met the aforementioned group who had gone the other way round. So in passing we had a long chat and lo and behold, he came from St Annes – very near where I used to live.

Leaving the road which was very noisy we entered a quieter scene with the cycle track among trees and fields,-with occasional derelict buildings and land bogged machinery gradually rusting away with weeds gradually growing and covering the mess. The track always had several people in view, those on bicycles creeping up silently – no bell ringing – you just had to keep aware. Sometimes you could see a long way ahead and other at times we were wondering what was round the next corner.

There were many families with all types of wheeled and brightly coloured pedalled conveyances travelling with great confidence, and others who persisted in walking while Mum or Dad carried a trike or bike in one hand and pushed a pram with the other. A Dad and three children came along and fancied our balloons, fortunately we had three and so they carried our message back along the track. One particular form of transport I saw was a scooter with both left and right footings – that's an idea!

The last part of our day became a walk behind several little towns on field footpaths. I thought we had reached the last one, where we were to have tea. Unfortunately it was Saturday afternoon and mums and toddlers were having a 'do.' But we did get a cup of coffee then I discovered it was not the end of our walk, but the next stop would be.

We landed up in a lovely extensive country park with a Golf Course and a Visitor Centre which was our goal. Then there were complications with our taxi followed by the taxi not being able to find us. Anyway it eventually did. We collected our own car and set off for the home run, still looking for somewhere to eat – not a good time for it was 5.00pm. Anyway after running through three villages Cath found the Black Bull, a little pub hiding behind another one in the main street. This was a good find and earned our full approval. We were shown through to the back which was quiet and had the menu, which was enormous, brought to us by the boss. He held it with both arms outstretched. We each had our own choice which was beautifully presented.

So now we had enough energy to get us home at 9.00pm but Cath and Geoff still had to continue on to get home.

Day 1 Wallsend to Tyne Bridge by Cath

Doris had timed her preparations to the minute, breakfasted, packed, and so it was we got told off when we arrived – forty minutes early! She was still in the bath! Kirkstone shrouded in fog but we were soon out of it and an excellent bright sunny day to Wallsend. As instructed I phoned Tony at Radio Newcastle and there he was, microphone in hand as we drove into Segedunum, kindly transported by Darren (Darren works on the helideck of oil rigs and we soon ascertained that he had been on Britannia Rig as had Geoff's son).

So the media frenzy of the Spider trek began! Julie from Look North was there with a big complicated video camera sprouting interesting appendages (the camera not Julie) Doris was very articulate as usual, I was pretty inarticulate and burbled things about the trek, missing vital bits of information, and so it went on.

We finally started walking at noon, waved off by Tim Brown's friends, his god-daughter and Trevor, the lovely manager of Segedunum. Passing children on a history trip with crayons and worksheets running happily across the Roman ruins near the restored bath house – along the former Blythe and Tyne Railway and a slightly bumpy beach made from old steel girders and patches of burnt tarmac thanks to bored pyromaniac youths.

Two miles of industrial land, past Rise and Shine Bakery from which emanated magnificent smells – reminded me that it was eight hours since breakfast at 5.00am. Another phone call – this time it was Centre- point wanted to tell me that Tyne Tees TV wanted to come and see Doris. I told them to rendezvous with us at St Anthony's Park in about ten minutes but Doris stopped to examine trees and flowers so by the time we got to the Park, the cameras were set up and ready to film us arriving. Nice friendly guys.

We approached the first of seven Tyne bridges in bright sunshine, the Sage shone like a sleek incandescent armadillo and - the locals call it the Slug – such a shame knowing what fantastic musical and artistic things go on inside.

A steep walk up to the station to find a bus for our overnight stop; we got in and with the grumpiest driver in Newcastle who mindlessly told us "Ee, 'tis not a reet gud area here-like...." Thanks, mate. The West Park Hotel is the ultimate bog standard accommodation about which I am not going to sully the pages of this book.... Blackfriars restaurant's evening meal was lovely, Tim B joined us again. I told the polite young Geordie waiter about the walk and he pressed some money into Doris's hand and wished her well. There was an ancient climbing creeper tree which spread its tendrils above our head and clung to the ceiling of the restaurant.

Day 2 Tyne Bridge to Tyne Riverside Country Park by Cath

After a hearty breakfast at Lloyds, The Quayside, attaching balloons to our rucksacks and taking a last look at the bridges, we set off west into a steady breeze, encountering fishermen, walkers, cyclists all doing their own Saturday thing, many of whom had seen Doris on TV the night before and stopped to chat and wish us well. Information boards now drew us into the world of ship building: Thomas Armstrong, the Japanese connection and we passed by the skeletons of many old boats and the impressive coal staithes across the water. Doris was fascinated by everything but especially by a flock of racing pigeons that had just been released from their lofts and were circling in perfect formation –whoosh, whoosh past us and then round again. Our path took us up Scotswood Road, of Blaydon races fame and several cars hooted and waved, a bus driver and cyclists waved – it must have been the balloons and Doris's green coat – instantly recognisable garb of a 95 year old TV celebrity. A small group of walkers stopped and asked what was by now the standard question. "Aren't you the lady on the telly last night?"

Guess where they were from – St Annes. Away from the busy road we sat down on a bench for a snack. A young man and three children came past eyeing up our balloons. I said "Do you like balloons?" and the littlest one said "Why aye" Bright even wider eyes as I gave it to him – two more pairs of eyes looked at the other two balloons. "OK would you like one each too?" "Oh, yes, please" "What are your names?" "Cain, Naomi and little Darren" he said. "Why little? You look big to me." I said. "Because he's Big Darren." pointing to the young man. Adults are so stupid sometimes!

We passed a steel sculpture that none of us could make sense of, but Doris banged a tune on it with her special stick. The Stick was beginning to have celebrity status of its own, thanks to the telly. Lemmington boasts a wonderful Children's Centre, with café, but as the law of sod dictates it was shut. A kind receptionist made us coffee and we set off for the last push to Riverside Park and the taxi back to Wallsend. The driver was an authority on all the former watering holes of the Scotswood Road but Doris didn't have a clue as to what he was talking about so just smiled politely.

A hearty meal at the Black Bull, Haltwhistle and we set off back to Ambleside. Kenny, the Tyne Tees reporter had asked me "Will she make it?" "No, question." I answered.

THE SECOND LEG

Male ladybird spider

Hadrian's Spider Trek Leg II by Doris

Riverside Country Park to Harlow Hill by Doris

We left about 1.00ish, Lorraine drove all the way- wonderful extensive views of rolling fields, not sunny but mostly fine. Stopped at a summit café for coffee - £8 for three coffees and one soup – then on to Haydon Bridge through Alston. There were beautifully appointed rooms with every possible drink, fresh milk and water. We had a good talk round the table in Michelle's room. Went to Co-op to buy food for tomorrow and bought batteries for Tim's camera. Nick has found a good pub for food later in the evening and we are to assemble at 6.15, very good.

Day 1 Riverside Country Park to Harlow Hill by Doris

The morning was fine and it was quite difficult to find the starting point which seemed to be miles back to our previous walk but eventually found a pleasant walk by the riverside. We met a local lady who had never ventured that far before but nevertheless told us which path to take. However, we soon came across enormous playing fields all sorts of goals etc., and a golf club. We rounded these and discovered Newcastle University Biological Station and lots of parked cars, then we wound up and up and up under the trees in the rain. We had to stop and draw breath, we had climbed that distant hill which lay to the left. Here we met Nick who had just ordered a meal in the café, so we had a coffee and a loo stop and later re-joined the path and carried on seeing a bit of the Wall on the way round the myriads of sheep in fields, over many stiles in mud and slippery stones, watching where we put our feet rather than the extensive views which we were passing through. Nick came and parked near a place we would be passing and we ate our sandwiches in the car. All very well satisfied and so back to the path, when we were near the day's finishing spot I got cramp – this slowed things down considerably but we DID make it to the end.

Day 2 Harlow Hill to Halton by Doris

Next morning our Mud Trek continued losing the rubber ferule on my stick continually, someone put their hands down in the mud to retrieve it. Muddy paths finally became grassy ones, all along the hedges which were the road boundaries – much better going. We saw wide vistas, storms in three or four different areas at a time, met a few people here, many doing different treks two men from Lincolnshire doing it the easy way- whatever that was! Ended up with a cluster of stiles, one after another then finally at the road to the castle, Nick was waiting by the big gates.

Preamble by Michelle

The next part of Doris' adventure and the beginning of ours started the day before walking began with tea and biscuits at Gatesgarth. It was a pleasure to see the amount of cards, well wishes and copious amounts of Hadrian's Wall literature around the house. Doris is definitely well researched and supported. So it was off to the accommodation for the night. The obvious need for copious amounts of coffee, tea and cake warranted stops at cute cafes on the way, one of which had breath-taking panoramic views of mountains rarely seen in Oxfordshire.

Day 1 by Michelle

We arrived at the Reading Rooms, a B and B in Haydon Bridge, to find we had taken over the whole three bedroom house. So, being the proud 'owners' of a new home for the next two nights we, of course, took it on ourselves to make it our own. One of the bedrooms had a great view of the river rushing through a weir, we moved around some of the furniture and set up a spot to sit down, chat and have some more - you've guessed it - tea! With the lovely view accompanying us, conversation ensued. Interesting topics kept arising as to be expected from three generations of vastly differing experiences. We attempted to explain exactly what the internet is, concluding somewhat vaguely that it is a telephone network with pictures. This soon moved on to the best\most influential invention of Doris' lifetime, the answer seemed to come easily: plastic. I had never contemplated a life without plastic as naïve as that might be. But quickly came to understand what a major development that was. Even Mum remembers being influenced by the invention as my grandfather worked at Dupont during his time in Seattle. Second best invention for Doris was – the washing machine. Dinner at the local pub was by anyone's standards huge, side dishes as big as the dish itself covered the table. It was definitely a good aid for a sound night's sleep before the walk.

Day 1 Tyne Riverside Country Park to Harlow Hill
by Michelle

The walk started very pleasantly along the river. The sun was hot, paved footpath under foot as we started off through the park. Three Centre Point balloons attached to Doris' rucksack meant she couldn't be missed. I believe it was a much calmer affair setting out compared to the first leg; no news teams this time. The Hadrian's Wall Path book became firmly attached to my hand over the next few days, I became accustomed to reading a map from right to left and made sure we did not stray from the strict instructions to follow the guide!

We were soon taken off the patch, out of the park and onto a ridge way, from here we could see Heddon-on-the-Wall up on the hill, knowing we soon had to conquer the incline. But by now you won't be surprised to hear Doris made it up without any issues and it provided a good spot to stop for coffee at the top and take in a pleasant view. We had passed a rugby club, golf club and Newcastle University Campus on the way up, before eventually getting into the village. They all seemed pretty accustomed to Hadrian's Wall tourists around here, very politely pointing us on our way. The tea shop was very busy too. There is a section of the wall still remaining in the village which provided the backdrop for our lunch Yes, we were fully fuelled by this point: tea, coffee, cakes, crisps and sandwiches consumed.

The second half of the walk was not so scenic and the clouds made an appearance. Mostly taken along busy roads we were encouraged by friendly beeps of motivation from the traffic. The rain began, but the waterproofs refused to come out, much to Mum's dismay. We started to meet other Hadrian's Wall challengers along the way, all doing it in different amounts; varying sections, time periods and direction. There were lambs in abundance with their mothers and a few cow fields, we had to take detours around, through endless kissing gates. The ground was quite uneven underfoot for the most parts and it was a relief to walk along the tarmac when it made its appearance. One last incline through a field took us to Harlow Hill. Dad waiting for us at the top with transport and stories of people he had spoken to who had heard of Doris' adventure in the media.

As for the Romans: we did cross through a fort of theirs along the way, Vindolanda, now fully covered. At least where we were walking it now, there were some lovely undulating bumps for sheep to graze and lambs to play. The guide book was helpful to bring the history to life. So with only a few cramps and one blister we headed back to the Reading Rooms, another huge dinner at the same place and bed.

Leg II Day 2 Harlow Hill to Halton by Michelle

Balloons re-attached, we set off once more, aware of what was ahead. Doris seemed used to the countryside setting, as from what I heard the first leg was quite different. Much of what followed along the road which in turn provided good chances for breaks at local pubs and tea shops dotted along the way. We noticed a lot more 'challengers' today. Some just out for a day's walk but many raising money for various causes. Two men were completing it in six days, another was going non-stop throughout the night! We had a chat with a few here and there, a good chance for photo opportunities, but no-one ever expected anyone of Doris's age to be doing it when we explained her adventure. The look on their faces was amusing and I felt very proud.

Sheep were a strong theme of the day being that they were everywhere. We stopped to watch one poor lamb's dilemma as it got stuck in the adjacent field to its mum. Curiosity having got the better of him, he climbed through a dividing gate. The amazing thing was that a different mum on the same side as the lamb saw what was happening, walked over and tried to open the gate to let him through. It didn't work but incredible to see the sheep recognise the problem, think of a solution and put it into practice. Sorry, sheep I just didn't think you were that clever! Impressed. Not so many obstacles for us today. Well, no uphill. Main challenges came from endless stiles, for which we developed a fool-proof technique towards the end; oh, and having to keep retying the balloons else Doris became engulfed by them, losing her head and becoming unrecognisable!

Just before the last approach to our finish line, we crossed through another fort which opened to great panoramic views. They sure knew where to place them. We couldn't help thinking that all the small hills and mounds looked great for riding a bike on. Then I noticed a point to point sign nearby and was happy to see others had similar ideas. So the final slight descent led us to the entrance of Halton Castle, our end point. Not without a few more stiles to negotiate first, of course. With that, chauffeured back by Dad, we were heading back to Ambleside.

It was a pleasure, wonderful experience and great fun to do this leg with Doris. Happy walking for the rest of the legs!

THE THIRD LEG

Peacock Spider

Hadrian's Wall Trek III Doris

Day 1 Harlow to Chollerford by Doris

Much upset re Taz: rang vet for emergency appointment, down to vet for 9.30. call had been transferred to Windermere – too early: vet very good, and left Taz to be cared for until I return: temperature 104. Tim landed up with Tis. So went back to town to see about opening Age UK on Friday. Michael, Gwyn and Chris arrived "bang on" sorted T-shirt's to be given. The party arrived on the dot. Gwyn drove all the way – fine, sometimes misty. Digs fair but pally hostess. Two bathrooms shared by the House, two gigantic baths, one had a loo and two washbasins, the other a loo, shower and washbasin, thousands of bottles, and so on. One big piece of soap was difficult to operate in the bath which had three plugs - lovely. I worked a necessary plan to manage carefully the entrance and hopefully exit, relief after it was over.

The walk was similar to last time especially the tree roots, stones and lots of mud. Stiles as before, fell twice, I didn't break anything. The track was extended by making a big detour round private grounds. We had tea then ice cream at two points on the way. Michael, an excellent leader, which made it interesting. I got slower and slower as we finished this detour. Gwyn supported me and we finally got back. 7 miles exhausted. The meal, last night in Hexham really good. Tonight we ate at the B and B, pretty good but very hard vegetables. They do an excellent line in fresh fruit salad here. Another group here last night collecting for renal cancer, we exchanged contributions. They worked at the Freeman Hospital where I went with my kidney stone.

Day 2 Chollerford to Old Repeater Station by Doris

We set off fine, walked right from the door. BUT bad weather forecast, fields, woods and stiles followed. Saw a really good part of the Wall, now raining, tripped over tree roots on the way, hurt ribs but could still continue. Weather got worse, rain and wind. Richard saw a barn ahead where we finally landed, TERRIBLE, no side walls, ground all churned up and farm machinery scattered about, impossible to sit or even lean. Ate a Penguin with much difficulty and drank my coffee. After we got home I discovered the others had managed to eat their packed lunch, other people in the same boat. Each decided the only thing to do was to carry on. Conditions are awful, deep areas of bog to cross, then the next similar; we searched for places to put our feet only to find the next bit just as bad

We were struggling in a bog then I stepped on what appeared to be a patch of firm reeds etc, fell in and Michael who was helping me fell on top of me. We were both soaked both inside and out. The others managed to keep their feet and looked back to see where we were. A decision was made to get onto the main road which ran alongside over a wall. We found a gate to do this. The road was very busy and each time a vehicle approached Gwyn and Michael pushed me onto the verge with our backs to the road. Eventually we arrived at the Old Repeater Station. Here we took off our outer clothing and bags into a drying room and were given a hot drink and a chocolate biscuit. I was shivering, my tongue too numb to speak coherently (I think Chris was shivering too). We sat close together in the car to keep warm on the way home – what an interesting walk this has turned out to be!

Leg III with Doris, Mike Arnott, Gwyn Abbott, Chris Stewart, Richard Arnott

Preamble: Mike and I drove up to St Annes from Colchester and thence to Ambleside to collect Doris. It was a good, if windy, drive from Ambleside to Walwick Farmhouse, our B and B for the night. It was into the clouds across the North Pennines and through bits of heavy rain. Margaret at the B and B welcomed us with open arms and showed us to our rooms. The view from the front of the farmhouse was wonderful, particularly when the sun shone, which it did for most of that evening. We all met up in our room which was the biggest and most palatial.

our bed !

Wetherspoons in Hexham for dinner, cheap and cheerful and enjoyed by all, I think.

Day 1 Harlow to Chollerford by Mike

Next morning Richard joined us for breakfast, having left Edinburgh at 6.00am! We all piled into our car for the ride to the start of Leg 3. Doris recognised the place, Halton Chesters, and we parked up and prepared ourselves. The walking was quite easy, across fields and through Stanley Plantation. We went over a lot of stiles and saw a variety of wild life and livestock. After a picnic lunch we went on towards St Oswalds, where there was the promise of a tearoom, very welcome, then on to Planetrees, which was the first close-up bit of the Wall we saw. After Planetrees the path did a big bend round Branton. A small road became a much larger one and we had to follow it as it led to a road over the River Tyne. Doris was beginning to tire and we had to hang onto her to stop her falling into the road. We finally made the river and found a heron fishing in the middle. The last bit of the day was a real slog up the road but everyone was happy, if tired. Then we reached the B and B at Walwick. Dinner in the B and B and early to bed with an unpromising weather forecast.

Day 2 Chollerford to Old Repeater Station by Mike

The next morning was damp with either heavy drizzle or heavy rain. After a good breakfast we got kitted out, and one car was taken to the Old Repeater Station. The trail went directly from the farmhouse across the fields and stiles.

Past Limestone Corner and Greencoats we were able to see bits of the Wall again. The ground became boggier and we got wetter. At Brocolitia Roman Fort we gave up trying to keep the bog out of our boots. We bashed on to Carrow Farm in spite of having no shelter and in a hungry state. We found a draughty empty barn where we ate our sandwiches standing up: too cold to linger so we went on slowly. The ground became boggier and boggier and Doris slipped bog-ward, Mike following to help her but he fell in too!

Stopping for the necessary – much easier for men than for ladies.
At the Old Repeater Station a very nice lady took pity on us, made us tea and coffee and let us remove some wet gear before setting off home.

THE FOURTH LEG

Struggling but still going

Hadrian's Spider Trek Leg IV

Day 1 Old Repeater Station to Once Brewed by Doris

This is the fourth leg with estimated mileages of 4.4 and 4.1. I had been looking forward to the trip as being the shortest of all and to be able to say we were half way through and the most difficult one completed. How wrong can you be!

We arrived at the starting point around lunch time so ate our lunch and then prepared for the walk, having had a pleasant journey via the Kirkstone pass and Alston. The memories of that particular spot were not good but conditions here were much more pleasant now, so we started. Quite early we missed the sign and had to enquire for the route – they told us a short cut round the back of the farm to join the path. It is interesting that we saw virtually no signposts or other means of guiding us as previously. This is owing to a change of management owing to the new county authorities. Also the endless stiles were absent, I think we only used three, which were not as high as those we had got used to and of very poor quality.

The going was good, but was tiring due to the undulating ground. Every time we achieved a climb up to a hill top ahead we were immediately faced with another just as high, but had first to descend to ground level again before we could start the climb. This continued until we finally descended, having another hill ahead, to find our digs. The weather was OK with only a little rain.

We met quite a few people walking in the opposite direction – two of them emptied their pockets for our funds. Later we met crowds of young adults walking quite fast to visit Housesteads. Continuing, we came to ground level again, which I thought was final, but no, we were off again along a very rough and narrow path alongside Crag Lough, up and down again with a precipitous and dangerous edge falling down to the Lough below. This finally ended with a very steep and rocky drop, higher than the highest part of Carver Church, and NO path. I wandered about along the top and didn't think I could descend even with help - if that were possible - and then decided IT MUST BE DONE, and went down on my bottom- choosing the best route on either side as I went – only possible if you have your two free arms. Phew! When I came home I told Tim, my neighbour, about this, it's called Cat Stairs on the map, and he replied "That's how I do it." So I felt better about it. After this we missed the track down to the main road and after some more very rough ground, finally thanks to the mobile we were picked up by Alison and Norman, and taken to our pub in Twice Brewed. We were supposed to dine at 7.00pm but we were allowed to make it 8.00pm. The pub was fine, everyone very friendly and generous.

When I went downstairs for dinner they offered me a better room but I had got everything sorted and didn't feel I could move again, so turned it down. After that I got lost in the maze of corridors and finally knocked several times on the door I thought was mine as I couldn't make the key work. Finally a naked man unlocked it and told me where to go – it was the boss's son!

Day 2 Once Brewed to Haltwistle by Doris

Morning came and I found myself half dressed on the bed and the light still on. My watch had stopped. Went downstairs to see what time it was –their clock had stopped too, so went to ask someone – there were not many people about. By now I knew that I was not going to be able to walk that day, I could only just manage the stairs.

We waited for ages for Hugh to arrive and then Alison did part of the walk and we went home. What do you think- the cat had been shut in the broom cupboard all the time I had been away. She was OK. I will tack this next part on to the end or some later date.

Day 1 Old Repeater Station to Once Brewed by Judith

Our section of the Spider trek began with a night at base camp with Chris in St Annes. We left on Wednesday morning to pick up Doris in Ambleside and then on to our starting point at the Old Repeater Station. It was an excellent beginning as we drove right past it and had to turn back a couple of miles.

By this time it was 12.15 so we ate our butties, blew up the balloons, kitted ourselves out and started walking. A helpful lady from the Old Repeater Station suggested we start up the road rather than the very boggy field. We lost the track but Peter found some farmers, either branding or castrating lambs, who pointed us in the right direction. Doris was not too happy with the first stile as it consisted of stones sticking out of the wall.

The first glimpse of the open landscape was glorious – wide and dotted with sheep and cattle and a profusion of buttercups. The path began fairly gently and we were strolling adjacent to the wall. This was a false impression!! The guide book described the walk as "undulating" but it omitted to say "severely." We later discovered that this is one of the most difficult parts of the Wall path and, though not long in distance, very steep and rugged in places. At one point, towards the end, the only way Doris could descend was on her bottom!

We took six hours to complete the so-called four mile trek and Doris was extremely tired by the end of the day. Fortunately we were in contact with Al and Norman who drove up a track to meet us and took us the last three quarters of a mile back to Twice Brewed Inn where we were staying overnight.

We did, however, have some interesting moments en route! The rain fell, the sun shone and the temperature fluctuated, becoming quite cold towards the end. We also found a large hole which may have been made by a badger. We met several interesting people: a Dutch lady on her own with walking stick and umbrella, a couple of men, John Gaves and Alec, with a c, from Lincolnshire who were walking fifteen miles each day in aid of African children. They also gave us all the change from their pockets. There was a huge bus load of students, possibly from Scandinavia, walking in the opposite direction to us.

That evening Al and Norman joined us for a meal at the Twicc Brewed Inn. The staff were extremely friendly and on hearing about Doris immediately put her on their face book page. She also caused havoc by mistaking a bathroom for her bedroom and trying to open the door while the owner's son was having a shower!

Day 2 Once Brewed to Haltwistle by Judith

We went downstairs to meet Doris for breakfast and her first words to us were "I'm not walking today." The previous day had been very tiring and she felt wobbly so came to a wise decision.

We were expecting Hugh to join us at 9.30 and Al had a text to say he was on his way! Al, Norman and the three of us sat and drank coffee, and by 11.15 we were still "waiting for Hugo." He arrived having left home in Durham at 9.30! Anyway he and Al went to suss out the next stage of the trek in July and we and Doris ambled our way back to Ambleside via the Old Vicarage at Beltringham where we spent two very happy New Years in 1997 and 1998. We're hoping to walk the lost stretch between Stone Rigg and Haltwhistle next year.

THE FIFTH LEG

Beaded spider – made of beads!

Hadrian's Spider Trek Leg V

Day 1 Haltwhistle to Gilsland by Doris

We gathered up in the car park. The going was pretty good throughout the walk. It was fine, or raining not too heavily, with grass and rushes most of the time. We had a short coffee break and a longer one for packed lunches, cake and biscuits. Unfortunately, at one point the party split, half deciding to keep up the hill and the rest to drop down across the hill-side to the farm, where a track began. Brian kept going between the two groups as neither wanted to undo the travelling that had been achieved. We were in the lower group and watched the others as they individually came down to join us. That was the worst bit of the day.

We soon stopped for lunch, which was rather wet. We had fun soon after where a man was rebuilding part of a damaged wall. The tractor-cum-dumper blocked the track, we had to go down one side of this, close under the main mass of the crane and on to the other side. We had a conversation with the worker, who was drenched, but happy enough filling in the centre cavity of the wall with very small stones. We were passing through the Northumberland National Park. The grass was being cut by at least two mowers, one a sit-on, and one by a girl. There were many wild orchids, various colours and types and other native plants. In the distance we saw water in an old quarry with ducks.

Norman appeared round the corner from the National Park Tea Room, somehow I was in front and with Norman entered the Tea Room – full of people standing round a long table. They sang Happy Birthday (much too early). The people were with the young folk from Centrepoint – Jennifer, the fundraising boss, and Shirley who read me a copy of a letter from Prince William. Graham had made a cake and there were also cup-cakes. I was asked to blow out the candle and cut up the cake. I handed it round and spoke to as many as I could, but the pieces got smaller and smaller. This was an unexpected shock! And we continued on our way.

Barbara left us. We waited until the evening meal began – trout, mange tout peas, four or five, and three or four small potatoes wrapped up in greaseproof paper and paper clips, a small apple crumble portion, custard or ice cream for those who wanted it. I spent a very hard night mostly awake with acute cramp (thinking no way could I walk next day.) I ate all my Kendal mint cake with water.

ST JAMES'S PALACE

Dear MR. Hancock,

    I was so incredibly impressed to hear that you are walking eighty-four miles along Hadrian's Wall, in aid of Centrepoint. As Patron, I could not be more grateful to you for taking on this huge challenge and raising so much money and awareness for homeless young people across England.

    I want to send you my very best wishes for the rest of your tremendous Spider Trek! I hope and believe your gardening training and walking stick will stand you in good stead along the way, not to mention all your wonderful friends and family who I know are supporting you.

With the best of luck!

William

Day 2 Gilsland to Banks by Doris

Next morning I warned them that I might not manage and not to worry if it happened. But to my surprise all was well – nobody more surprised than me!

It took us ages to make our departure. We followed instructions, ate our lunch on the roadside and later had a cup of coffee in Meg's café at Gilsland, called House of Meg. We walked a bit further, then split up and re-gathered at the car park. We were home by 6.00pm: very good time and driving.

Doris accepted a lift to avoid the last steep descent and ascent to the finish at Birdoswald. Later in the year she went back with friends to complete the missing bit "Because that's not right."

Birdoswald to Banks by Barbara

We parked at Banks East Turret and caught a service bus to Birdoswald Fort. With us were Jane Pilgrim and her 19year old nephew from Australia. For much of the way we enjoyed extensive views both north and south with remains of the accompanying ditch or vallum clearly visible. We made good progress until we came to the inevitable and unavoidable patch of mud. The field wall offered some support while William chivalrously placed his foot for Doris to use as a stepping stone! Friendly ponies, perhaps hoping for some goodies, welcomed us at the final stretch, but they were unlucky and we kept our lunch to eat sitting on the Wall at Banks. A short car journey took us back to Birdoswald Fort where William explored the extensive ancient remains while we three enjoyed a relaxing cup of coffee in the café.

Day 1 Haltwistle to Gilsland by Alison
The Exotics Cavalcade no less than six of Doris' friends...

The nickname for this leg came after Cath and I saw the film, The Exotic Marigold Hotel, and with all of us being of pensionable age, we could not avoid a wee giggle at the possible similarity. It's definitely a must for Doris to see.

This leg of the Spider trek became very popular for Doris's friends to walk with her – a summer's walk. Some logistics for a rendezvous at the start began to take on a military dimension as we gathered from different points in Ambleside, Windermere, St Annes (via St Andrews, Dorothy and Derek, and us from Highland Perthshire. We all miraculously arrived at Caulfield car park within minutes of each other – so with the rain starting, there was donning of waterproof trousers and jackets (except Doris), issue of Kendal mint cake supplied by Doris, general meeting and greeting, coffee and fruit cake to set us on our way with brollies up and Doris looking very fetching in mini sou'wester.

The cavalcade finally left the car park at 10.20 with Norman plus the dogs, Jake, Kate and Lucy, staying as a back-up car to rendezvous at the planned café at Walltown, or sooner if anyone needed it or the rain became unbearable! With contingency plan in place for a reason to become evident we reached the start of the path - to be faced with a stile of Roman proportions, which we had to negotiate to get into the field. Doris took one look and stated "Huh, I don't like the look of that!"

However, we eventually got over it and set off up the path on a gentle incline. Aesica fort was the first architectural point of interest, although it was so wet, no-one wanted to get the book out to find the details. The white horses grazing in and around the fort caught Doris's eye as she really likes horses.

The Cavalcade pushed on and despite Doris insisting it wasn't raining that much, when I removed the golf umbrella I held over her most of the day, she did admit it was. In fact Barbara noted the 'balloon music' was an interesting accompaniment to the day, as raindrops fell on the Centre Point balloons behind our backs.

We took the chance to turn and face the east and admire the distance Doris had already covered since those two dry days in March when she, Cath, Geoff and Tim left Segedunum. Doris took on a new persona with eight of us strung out on the path – Mother

Hen. She was constantly doing a head count to make sure we were all there. There were some vey splodgy sections both on the level and on inclines, but with Brian and Barbara doing a bit of trail blazing we managed to suss out the most accessible- or just less slithery bits of the path. We had some great bits of wall beside us on the first section and we were constantly amazed at the work involved not only in bringing the stones to the site but the work in dressing them to the rectangular or square shapes needed long before any of the lifting or cutting gadgets we have now. It might have been a hare- brained plan but siting it on the precipitous crags we were passing on our right. Hadrian certainly was a good one.

We had a coffee stop in the only bit of woodland on this section and the Exotics were intrigued by a triangular, collapsible seat I had in my rucksack for Doris, provided by Norman who swears by it. However, Doris preferred the security of terra firma and her little sheet of plastic which she produced, I suspect it is a piece of an old plastic mac in the true economic, recycling fashion of Doris.

Bryan who is of considerable stature decided to keep me happy and perched on the seat seeing as I'd brought it. We had an ongoing challenge to keep the balloons attached, clearly our knots did not reach Guiding standard, or was it the slippery round cord which Barbara found which did not hold tight?

As we approached Walltown Crags, I knew from my recce the previous month that this would involve a precipitous descent on steps with no handrail and another climb up so had sussed out a safer lower route for Doris which D and I headed for, as the others had stayed up higher. However, Mother Hen became a bit disconcerted at this point, observing that this was the first time on the whole walk that the group had been split, but neither had there been such a big group before. I hopefully reassured her that we would soon regroup.

We passed an isolated farm with very neat grass – a bit out of context in the wilds but we stopped to admire it and observed that there must have been sun at one time as there was an upturned garden chair in the garden and perhaps one sat in it occasionally? The inquisitive, probably hopeful for food, sheep (Doris said they had blue Leicester in them) were intrigued by these strange looking women. They had extraordinarily long wool a bit like a loose Rastafarian and one shook just like a dog coming out of a river as they were so soggy. Perhaps it was my big brolly they envied?

We were by now walking more easily on a farm road - even tarmacked - and very shortly the splinter group made contact, first by mobile, then immediately they spotted us below, due to balloons, and we saw them waving, or doing semaphore with a brolly – on the skyline at the top of the field we were walking through. Relief for Mother Hen indeed! They descended to meet us, as we stood and sussed out a lime kiln as a possible lunch-time site. And discarded it, due to the less-than–stable stonework and moved on to shelter under a huge oak tree.

Lunch was welcomed by all so out came the little mats, D's plastic mat, boxes of food: rucksacks seemed to take on the guise of a tardis! Dorothy was getting down to sit on the ground and before we knew it she nearly fell into Doris' lap as she put her hand on the plastic sheet and slid down hill slightly. Great hilarity and she was yanked back up as I managed to catch her.

Doris was aware of my mobile going off quite a bit all morning. I had to say it was Norman checking up, but with an extra dimension which would soon be revealed! However, as the rain continued to drip through the tree we set off again fairly smartly – only to be faced with a huge tractor with a front bucket blocking the path. It was the farmer repairing a bit of broken wall (farm, not Hadrian's Wall) and it was the easiest way to transport his stones. However, he had no intention of shifting so we squeezed between it and the wall under the arm of the bucket loader! Doris, Barbara, and I managed this and one or two others but the next thing we saw was Dorothy crawling under the bucket, or trying to. She hadn't realised that we had all walked under the arm. She didn't get right under fortunately, as many yells made her reverse.

After these interesting diversions, the route took us round a large pond at Walltown Quarry, which had been reclaimed and developed into a walking area, car park and café. Barbara spotted an orchid, then many more were spotted so a photo opportunity was seized. We leant on the wall surrounding the pond, which was more or less covered with lilies, with a narrow channel which Doris thought was kept open by the large flock of ducks swimming to and fro in the manner of ice-breakers at the Poles. Swifts were having great fun diving and swooping around too.

By this point our wonderful support team member, Norman, was to be seen waving as we rounded the corner and walked with us to the café and the sheltered rest area, which was a welcome sight and had been eagerly anticipated for some time.

What a total surprise for Doris as she walked into the café to be greeted by a group of people singing Happy Birthday, and cakes and balloons on the table, all organised by Jennifer from Centrepint!! What left Doris almost speechless (though not for long) was Shirley from Centrepoint reading out a personal message from their patron, Prince William, thanking her for her amazing fundraising and wishing her a happy birthday too!! Even though I knew this was happening, hence all the calls during the morning. I still had a lump in my throat at the surprise and delight this brought to Doris, all of which was captured by the Tyne Tees camera crews for the 6.00pm ITV news.

We were all pretty wet, so the break, with tea and cakes, was very welcome. The crew interviewed Doris and some of the young folk, especially Graham who had baked the cake the previous evening:

the first he'd ever made, he said, "A total inspiration!" Doris said "How right!" this clip was included in the broadcast report too. He's a lovely Geordie lad, who would be moving into his own flat two days later, which is a great example of the kind of work Doris is raising money for. After much filming and cakes Doris and the Cavalcade decided that this was enough for one day especially in those conditions so Norman, the chauffeur, orchestrated another, no, the first multi-car shuffle, which eventually delivered Doris, Timothy, Bryan and me to Bush Nook, our lovely B and B, and also returned the drivers plus Cornelia to their cars at the start. We could not have done this leg without him. Soon all the Exotics were drinking coffee and tea, courtesy of cheery Irish Malcolm: except Barbara who left us to visit her brother near Hexham.

Knowing that Doris was to be on TV sometime after 6.00pm, we at Bush Nook all got dried and changed and regrouped in the sitting room of the apartment where Doris, Norman and I were staying to wait for our now-famous friend to appear on screen. It was a good long piece, the two Ds exclaimed afterwards. "Ooh, didn't I look bedraggled!" "Yes, but all in a good cause." Luckily Cath, who sadly was not with us on this Leg was able, through the wonders of the internet to find links to the report so she could share in the amazing meeting at Walltown. Malcolm's son, Stephen, prepared supper – trout in brown paper, literally - and then he announced that he had a 'procurement issue' over the custard for the apple pie so only three of us could have it, the rest were with ice cream, neither of which Doris had, of course. And so to bed after a happy eventful day.

Day 2 Gilsland to Banks by Alison

We were promised by the weather man that Thursday would be better and it was. Unfortunately Doris had been awake a lot of the night with sore legs, but by the time we all gathered for breakfast she felt OK and said she would like to do some walking, in her usual determined manner. So it was agreed we'd take it in stages, as Norman and I had sussed out good car access points close to the wall on this section. Fortified by a good breakfast, with all six of us having a slight variation on the full English, we were ready to hit the trail. Mother Hen was slightly concerned at the head count and the two empty places at the table. Malcolm had forgotten that Derek and Dorothy were staying elsewhere, although they had eaten dinner with us last night.

Regrouping the Cavalcade, paying bills, positioning cars for the end of the day etc., all took some time but it was dry as we all set off from the previous day's finish point with no brollies, no sou'westers in use. Hooray! Military planning, however, was employed again as there was no mobile on this stretch - shock, horror! - but we managed. We were rewarded at the start by magnificent views of the rolling Northumberland landscape which we had missed the previous day. Doris was somewhat relieved to start the day by going through a gate, not a stile, of which there had been many the previous day. But most of the gates had muddy puddles beside them, which required some interesting balancing acts to get through. Doris proved herself very adept at this, often finding her own line of approach.

The first stretch was along a good section of the vallum, which I kept pointing out, and Doris said "You like that word, don't you?" There were peaceful cows lying around us as we walked down the slope, even the bull, who had his ladies, was quite unperturbed. I was much relieved. We also had great views of the crags below the wall both at Steel Rigg, the end point of Leg IV day 1, and Walltown. We passed a small group of women who were doing the walk in preparation for the Great Wall of China! Oops, I forgot to write in yesterday's notes that the one group we chatted to yesterday, going East was a German family who had done part of the Pennine Way and were on the Wall path where they coincide. Doris then told me that her grandfather was German, something I hadn't known before, and recited his long German name. Cath had

45

also found it as she did some genealogical research for Doris. It was so wet yesterday that we didn't chat that much.

As we came to the end of the first field, guess what, there was a stile, but luckily a gate too which was most unusual and worthy of another artistic attempt. As we rounded the path down to Thirlwall Castle in sunshine, we were met by Norman plus three dogs which was lovely – much meeting, greeting and patting ensued. Norman was going to go back and round by car to meet up at the bus stop, not for a bus but a coffee stop and the dogs made it quite clear that they wanted to walk with the exotics! So they were allowed to, especially as I was not holding the golf umbrella today: just walking with Doris. The path officially continued a short way along the road then up some deep steps to regain the field path but on our recce Norman and I had got permission from the farmer to go through their yard for this little bit. It went past the Golf Club where one of two men challenged Brian for walking up the track (I guess he'd lost his match!) but Brian politely told him we had been given permission for one day.

Quick rewind to our coffee stop which was beside some formed railway cottages, having negotiated a level crossing on the path. We noticed some lovely tiny blue flowers in nooks and crannies of the wall which was our seat. Of course it was Doris who named the flower – campanula. Back on the track which after a tricky wooden bridge surrounded by, yes, more mud, followed the vallum again. It was a gentle walk, but we rose towards a gate where the old fort had been, it became more challenging to avoid the slithery muddy path. We had to traverse a grassy slope. Doris managed it beautifully, with me just behind and hand from above plus, of course, her trusty stick carefully planted before she took any step Dorothy had slightly less success, but managed with quite a lot push/pull from the others. We were relieved, to put it mildly, to find ourselves on a level stretch once through the gate. There was our next Norman rendezvous point as we were close to Gilsland. I thought we'd have a break as it was nearly lunch time.

Alas, our meticulous planning fell apart as Norman had parked at the next access point.

So, once again the Cavalcade began to splinter: Doris and Bryan perched on a stile, I ran down the road to find Norman, feeling like an Army recruit at boot camp running with a rucksack and heavy boots, while the others set off along the path. Being warm and sunny it was hard work running and by the time I reached the car it was locked up, in the shade with the dogs but no Norman. With no mobile signal I just set off along the vallum to find him. By the time I did he was nearly back to where Doris and Bryan were. So I exchanged my rucksack for the car keys and ran back to the car and was able to pick up Doris and Bryan. All ended happily as the eight of us sat on the benches at the bus stop at Gilsland to have lunch in the sun: very leisurely. Some of us even applied sun tan lotion to our faces, poohed-poohed by Doris needless to say.

We all agreed that a proper coffee stop at the House of Meg in the village was a good idea and Doris treated us all to a delicious coffee and an ice cream for Norman. Thank you, Doris. Brian also had an Eccles cake and a discussion ensued between him and Bryan as to the source of the best ones. Bryan was adamant that M &S were the best ones. But the highlight of this stop (apart from the good coffee) was Brian discovering a plastic crocodile head, the jaw opened to reveal a set of teeth in the lower jaw. And, of course if you press certain teeth the jaw snaps down – so much jesting and giggling. Has the sun gone to our heads totally?

Back to the walk and we had an easy stroll along to Willowford Farm, beside one of the best sections of the Wall we'd seen on this leg. The line actually went down into the valley of the River Irthing, then up the escarpment to join at Birdoswald fort, but this would be very steep at the end of a second day. So Doris and I went round by car to meet the Intrepid Exotic Cavalcade at Birdoswald car park. There had been a tiny signal on the phone at this point and I had a message from Chris, the Press Officer at Centrepoint in London, as Radio Cumbria now wanted to do a phone interview with one hardy walker. However, after much cutting out of signals, we finally agreed that they would ring her at home tomorrow. This indeed happened after much hanging around on Doris's part waiting for the clarion call. As a postscript Cath was visiting Chris on Friday they had a call from Dorothy Tatton, one of the Exotics, who'd heard it announced when it would be broadcast so Cath and Chris were able to listen in too. Where will Doris's fame stop?

Back to the Wall and the rest of the Spider trekkers who all arrived safely at Birdoswald declaring it was very sensible for Doris to have nipped round by car as it was a long way down to the river. I actually walked back that way to Gilsland with the dogs so I know. So with another multi car share shuffle everyone was reunited with their cars and bags thanks again to Norman. We all went our separate ways home, tired but happy after an amazing two days with Doris on her Hadrian's Wall Spider Trek. The fundraising at this point is now over £3,000, much of it raised by Doris herself at various events. It is totally amazing and little wonder that when Centrepoint told the Palace about her, Prince William was keen to send a personal message.

So, Doris, strong boots and legs and may fair weather be with you for the final three legs.

THE SIXTH LEG

Cobalt Tarantula

Hadrian's Spider Trek Leg VI

Day 1 Banks to Walton by Doris

There were five of us: Ian, Richard, Barbara, Tim and me. Leaving home at 8.15, all was fine until we had to find the café in Walton where we were meeting. Eventually we discovered, there was no sign or indication that this was 'it' as it looked like the back entrance to an extinct village hall, the others were already wondering what had happened to us. We had a coffee and collected our packed lunches – a big roll, that's it!

We set off to find the place to park which Richard had already investigated. However, we found an unfriendly lady, who said her neighbours would very much object to us being there, adding that she herself was a good contributor to Centrepoint. So far this is the only person we met who was not pleasant.

This leg was to be different in many ways, there were no stiles but many kissing gates designed to make it easy for rucksacks on our backs. There were more cows than sheep, mostly beef herds of young bulls – half grown. Hens were good on this trip keeping their areas free of all crumbs, and begging from Richard for more, which he gave them. We met three different breeds of hens during the day.

A noted shop was one consisting of two sheds behind a hedge, stocked with Wall memento gifts: tops, caps, bags and sandals as take home gifts, all very good quality but expensive. There was no-one about at all, you just took your item and left the money in the box. Later we found a similar set up by a gate after a rather difficult and long traipse. There was a substantial lidded box containing various drinks, chocolate bars and biscuits – again

'Help yourself and leave the money', just what you wanted at this stage.

The walk was mostly on fields, the ground very wet and squelchy. Carlisle Airport was visible with loads of trucks, carrying cars in transport. We had lots of heavy rain but we each had brollies so that was fine. At lunch time we were fortunate to find enough stumps of trees to sit on and were joined here by Alison and Cath in their yellow gear for doing the Hadrian's Wall cycle Trek. It took a long time to eat the whole filled baguette we had purchased. We did very well on this level area and decided to do some of tomorrow's trek as we were well on time. However, torrential rain finally won the day and the farmer offered to take us in his truck to our evening B and B – we didn't ask – he just did it, all in the day's work.

Our accommodation was VG. I had a vast bathroom to myself, just opposite my door, with dressing gown provided. This had been a special birthday present from the owner to his wife. It was really indescribable. Every convenience you could think of all of the most up-to-date design and of course, spotless. I feared to mar it. However, there was no chair in my room, so Barbara lent me one of hers. Al and Cath met us at the local for an evening meal. And so to bed.

Day 2 Walton to Crosby on Eden by Doris

Next day was to be short – Richard went back to collect yet another baguette each, then we walked along similar ground to yesterday, saw two grey ponies in a field with impossible grazing, and a flock of hens enclosed in a very large cage with a low roof and very dark. We had walked for what seemed like miles and miles, looking for a place where we could sit and eat our 'B' food. We were near to the end now and soon reached Barbara's parked car, so we drove off, dropped the lads by their car and got home about 4.30.

Motto of this leg for the remainder of the trip – "Be sure you get a hard to eat baguette, then you will get sufficient rest."

Day 1 Banks to Walton by Ian

We had arranged to meet for an early start at the Rambling Rose Tea House at Walton Village Hall – an oasis of country culture where, in a converted classroom, locals and passers-by are provided with refreshment and recuperation. Ric and Ian arrived first, having travelled from Sheffield early to miss the congestion and chaos of the M62/61 rush hour. No sooner had their breakfast of fried egg sandwiches and coffees been served when Tim arrived followed closely by Doris and Barbara. Although Doris declined any further refreshment the rest of us took this opportunity to stock up on carbs and coffee.

With Doris's star status within the region (in no small part due to her frequent broadcasting opportunities) the proprietors of the café, Andrew and Denise, made an instant donation to the designated charity, Centrepoint.

Having finished breakfast we collected, or pre-ordered, lunches and left one car at the café (our finishing point for the day) and piled into Barbara's car. Despite dyslexic map reading by Ric we did manage to get to our start point: Banks, where Ric had already identified a parking place. Ric, ever the gentleman, checked with a resident who said, quite assertively, that our parking spot really ought to be somewhat further up the road. Ever keen to keep the peace our cars were relocated.

We're off! Down the hill to meet our first feature of the day Hare Hill, a short length of the Wall standing 8' 10'' high. Once thought to be the highest remaining piece of Wall left on the trek, it is now widely believed to be little more than a nineteenth century reconstruction using original Roman stones. Tim and Ian eventually found the small Roman inscription indicating that Primus Pilus, a senior centurion of the first cohort built it. In fact this stone was taken from a site called Moneyholes, some distance to the west.

Onward along the footpath, which is located parallel to the original Wall, past unseen but described turrets 53A and 53B over Craggie Hill through flocks of sheep down to Haytongate. Here a much publicised and used snack hut sits by the path. The hut even has its own website (www.itrod.co.uk.) Doris and Barbara admired some of the Hadrian Wall themed tee shirts that were on sale. Over-fed and very tame chickens met us as we went in, and pleaded with us to be fed as we went out. Ric, always a sucker for two legged or feathered things treated them to a small pack of garibaldi biscuits.

Moving on down past Abbey Gills Wood to Burtholme Park and over and up Garthside, we moved into fields of livestock, eventually stopping near Turret 55, where someone had conveniently left an array of felled trees which served as seats for our communal feast. Walton Café had provided baguettes filled with coronation chicken, ham and pickle which were devoured gratefully by all. The sharing of apple juice brought about the discovery that the fruit cake had been left in the boot of Ric's car at Walton, but the torpedoes seem to have more than satisfied all appetites.

Whilst enjoying our rest amid the rural and idyllic scene we soon became aware that our visual senses were being molested by what can only be described as oscillating, fluorescent aggravations in the distance. They seemed to be getting bigger and moving our way. Relief, as it was realised that it was only Cath and Alison, who had been cycling the Wall and had agreed to meet up with us. They were both dressed in bright yellow waterproofs which did nothing to flatter but everything to cover. As ever, Cath was overheating, she stopped and at once stripped to the minimum. Alison soon followed and they both took a break with us before continuing their journey towards Walton and their lunch. Break over, we continued onwards across Dovecotes Bridge to Walton. The path used to follow the line of the Wall to the ruins but for the last two years walkers have been encouraged to take what they say is a 'temporary' diversion along the road.

Arriving once more at Tea House in Walton we were greeted by the fluorescent duo who had just polished off a plate of this and a helping of that. We all settled down to tea and cake to celebrate the end of the first day. Doris was having none of this and wanted to continue further as it was only early afternoon. Refreshed and raring to go we decided to see if we could manage the next stretch to Newton farm, our accommodation for the night. Doris, Barbara, Tim and Ian set off on foot whilst Ric drove round to the farm to walk back towards us and, hopefully, meet half way .After a brief trek along the road past small houses and bright coloured gardened bungalows we were soon back in the fields. The terrain dropped through more farmyards to follow approximately the line of the Roman ditch. Crossing a small stream the path climbed through the woods to Sandygate, a gorgeous working farm.

From Sandygate we didn't follow the original Wall but seemed to be directed around field boundaries, through cow fields dropping to a second slightly larger stream with a series of little waterfalls. Cam Beck could be spied through the trees.

Here we met up with Ric. Having regrouped and walking further it soon became apparent that Doris needed to stop and rest. After a meeting in the farmyard at Cambeckhill Farm it was agreed to sit Doris down in a dry barn while Ric returned to collect the car to ferry Doris to our overnight stay. The local farmer was having none of it and was soon whisking Doris and Barbara to Newtown in his 4x4! Ric, Ian and Tim continued on foot across the fields and then up (more of this Later) to our B and B in Newtown.

Once we were all at Newtown, Ric took Barbara and Tim back to pick up their cars. Tim went onwards to Newcastle where he was meeting friends for the evening. Doris and Ian waited in the guest house sitting room, a comfy respite from the day, leafing through magazines and reflecting on the day. Newtown Farm bed and breakfast is a family run farm located directly on Hadrian's Wall on the site of the vallum. The stone buildings on the farm date back to 1772. We were soon settled in Doris with a bedroom which had a bathroom which was huge. Barbara was in a room which had more beds than she could handle and Ian and Ric shared a triple with décor straight from Lark Rise.

After showers, snoozes and baths we all met up at 7.00 to drive down to the Salutation Inn for our evening meal. This was recommended by all the guides and had a good write up in Trip Advisor. We had booked a table for six so Cath and Ali could join us for a night out on the town. From the outside it looked nothing special but inside it seemed to be split into three parts, a restaurant with the décor of an 80s Trust \House Forte dining room, a bar area where there were no nooks and crannies but clean lines and minimum bar furniture and games area for punters to play pool and darts.

While Ric went off to collect Cath and Al from their lodgings the rest viewed the menu plus a blackboard gave ample choice for all. Once we were assembled decisions were made. Ric was the only one not to have a pudding as the rest of us decided on the option of pudding. Doris wanted the prawns and creamy starter as a main course and this came as such amplified in size, Barbara and Ian opted for the slow cooked lamb steak or it could better be described as the family roast – huge portions. Ric went all Caribbean and ordered a Cajun salmon while Cath and Ali favoured pork medallions. Puddings were far more adventurous as a range of sticky, chocolate-covered, cream-enhanced concoctions were devoured by all except Ric. We all finished off with coffee or tea and the familiar chocolate mints. It was a fine evening, a fine meal all in fine company. Cath and Ali returned to their B and B via the help of the landlady's son. The landlady had decided it might be useful for him to become the local taxi driver so as to earn a few bob. So the newly developed talents of this young man were summoned by phone by Cath and Al. We left them in his capabale hands and headed off back to our own B and B, full, warm and ready for sleep.

Day 2 Walton to Crosby on Eden by Ian

Having all slept well, we awoke to a bright new morn of rain, rain and more rain. Breakfast was a scrumptious affair of bowls of fresh fruit, crunchy cereal, home cooked fry-up and warm toast washed down with coffee you could stain a parquet floor with. Ric went with Barbara to leave her car to our end point for the leg at Crosby-on-Eden, and returned to Newtown farm. Ric dropped the rest of us at Cambackhill Farm before driving to pick up our pre-ordered lunches while Barbara, Doris and Ian returned from our drop off point the previous day to Newtown.

Initially the walk was across fields and then upwards climbing a steep hill into the village of Newtown – distance-wise not very far. However, the hill was so steep that well placed steps had built in a continuous pattern right up the hill to the top. Doris admitted that she wouldn't have made such a climb the previous day and was glad to have attempted it this morning.

Once back in Newtown we met up with Ric already walking towards us. Packed lunches loaded we all ventured forth across the road and along the top of the plateau towards Old Wall. The overnight rain had soaked the fields and filled any vacant little ditch and flooded any field hollows. Consequently much testing of squelch levels was to occur throughout the day as our party now parading like a Jack Vettriano painting complete with sheltering umbrellas walked along the course of the ditch parallel to the vallum.

A whole patchwork of fields was crossed as we made our way towards Carlisle, a city whose highest buildings started to appear on the horizon. We walked with the ditch to our left and the curtain wall to our right. At Old Wall any of the original Roman structure had been swallowed up by the farm and outbuildings now on the site. The path continued straight through to Bleatarn Farm where some local school children had designed some information boards for walkers. Here we were to discover that Bleatarn, only a grassy mound of lumps and bumps was where the Roman soldiers used to quarry stone for the Wall – hence the 'tarn' now well grown over with reeds. At this point Carlisle Airport is away to the South. We kept seeing small planes taking off as the main airport was hidden by some huge distribution building, somewhat out of sorts with the rest of the environment.

Making good progress we made it to Wall Head where the Roman ditch becomes modern day tarmac. Here we tuned off to join a 'clarty' (local name for muddy) bridleway inappropriately named Sandy Lane. This leafy path eventually led after much analysis and examination provided an excellent bank – a dry slope of grass on which we could sit and enjoy our lunch. This time the fruit cake was not forgotten. Following lunch it was a short trek down and over via footbridge to the main A689 Carlisle to Brampton road where we picked up Barbara's car. The Drive back along the main road to our starting point seemed a noisy short affair. We arrived back in Newtown bade our farewells and returned to our homes.

THE SEVENTH LEG

Red Kneed Tarantula

Hadrian's Spider Trek Leg VII

Day 1 Crosby on Eden to Carlisle by Doris

9.00am was the departure time on this Leg- Tim and Jo for the first half, and Tim and Lis for the second. We returned home between the two days so there was no overnight stay. The first half was uneventful, finding the exact spot where we left off last time, messing about a bit on the way as there several Crosbys on Eden, Higher etc. It was not raining and we attacked a muddy route followed by a section along the road and over the M6. Here were interesting smells noted in "the Book 2" which we couldn't miss. There was an eccentric estate which had every possible kind of architecture that exists as well as several imposing entrances and a sculpture which made on the upper half of a felled tree, also odd bits of machinery scattered about.

The latter part of the day's walk was fairly easy and we finally arrived at the back of the Sands Leisure Centre co-ordinating with the end of a school day. Many very well dressed and well behaved boys flooded inside to get bites of various kinds with their pocket money, then home.

Day 2 Carlisle to Beaumont by Doris

This half of the Leg was to be a different matter altogether. Lis came to Gatesgarth and Tim picked us up as arranged, we were to meet Hannah from the BBC. She couldn't be found, then Tim came back and said she a bad migraine and was being sick. She said she would come in half an hour and she would say whether she could manage it. So! we coffeed, Tim went to look for her, it turned out that she was in the toilet and could come. I could not think why she needed to walk with us quite a way and then do the interviews.

She was dressed in a knitted shoulder cape with very expensive black trousers and what looked like little court shoes which she said were wellies (the tops, of course under the trousers) So we started, Tim carrying part of her apparatus. All this time it was slowly raining. So we started off, very pleasant walking in the vast National Park and golf course. We had taken a wrong turning and landed up behind the castle so we had to walk back and take the right turning) it was sign posted). After quite some time, Hannah decided it was time to do the interview. It was still raining and we were surrounded by beautiful trees in varying colours with the sodden, muddy path in the centre. It took ages. She screwed and unscrewed the legs of her camera and bent them, then put the camera on top, adjusted it, covered it over to keep off the rain, then made a hole in it so the lens could operate. Next there were more adjustments to the camera doing each one separately, then going round again to check etc, etc. Then we were ready – me first "what is your name?" etc, the simplest of questions, that had all been answered before, then Tim, then Lis. We walked a bit further, then had our lunch.

What had looked like a lovely walk beside the winding river on the map, turned out to be the complete opposite. The river was many feet below as the path was a series of steps down to water level (some with rails and some without), then few paces and back up again to path level, this was repeated time and again – they were all very long tiers of steps, the longest with forty nine steps. Not easy! Unless it was part of a public footpath it was muddy and raining on and off.

We went through a kissing gate into a field, this track, which was invisible, led to another kissing gate which could not be seen. The whole field was deep mud, we went from one spot to another trying to get through, sinking in over our boot tops, to and fro we went seeking possible routes ahead, but 'no' just as bad. Tim and Lis started collecting stones and placing them as steps but they just went down under as we stepped on them. We saw another party doing the same. There seemed to be no way we could get out of the field then Lis and I saw a rickety fence, Tim had managed to find a plank, if we could manage to get onto it we might escape – not that easy. With Tim's feet and some of the large collected stones. So I put my foot where Tim's was and then couldn't get the other foot out – they both hauled me out with great strength, I finally got on the plank and one by one we got on the fence, second rail up and sidled along to the gate which was slightly higher ground and with great care made it. As the road was near Lis and I sat in the wall, while Tim went to get the car. We had been a full hour trying to extricate our selves and the estimated 4.7 miles had taken us six hours. So that was the seventh leg done!

Day 1 Crosby on Eden to Carlisle by Tim

It was a beautiful sunny morning when we left house in Ireby to pick up Doris. Tim had already had one walk with the dogs, Hobbs ('Mr' Hobbs) and Ginni while Jo prepared a sumptuous picnic; pizza, chicken butties, ham butties and KitKats.

With Doris on board we set off up the drive full of excitement and had a beautiful drive through the lakes to Crosby on Eden, and Low Crosby twice, where we finally parked and started the walk. To be honest it was pretty uneventful, beautiful weather, reasonable paths, only one field containing a bull, cows and some mud and wonderful company. I really enjoyed walking and chatting to Doris while Tim walked with the dogs to and from the car, moved the car, walked back to join us for lunch on a very nice table on a green at Linstock. He then moved the car again to the Sands Centre in Carlisle, as recommended by another walker we met, and walked back to meet us again! After gently walking through Rickerby Park we walked close to the Eden and into Carlisle a welcome coffee and cake! Lovely day!

Day 2 Carlisle to Beaumont by Tim

There are many adjectives which can be used to describe this day, eventful, hectic, enjoyable, slow, but probably the most suitable one would be wet or muddy. Jo had seen the weather forecast the day before and gallantly gave way to Lis Mullen to allow her to enjoy the delights of the Carlisle area at its most damp. Lis made her own way to Chateau Doris in the morning ready for a prompt getaway at 9.00am.

As the BBC Look North East team which turned out to be one, were due to meet us at the off, we had a hectic two car chase up to and a cross Carlisle to leave one car at Beaumont, and then take the other to the Sands Leisure Centre stop point. We set off to sands in good style before turning round as Tim had left his boots in the car. Initial thoughts of 'it'll be OK in trainers' were fortunately ignored and a quick about turn was made. We arrived at Sands at the pre- arranged time exactly to see the BBC girl, Hannah, just pulling into the car park. Then it started to go wrong. Hannah told us she had a migraine, was feeling sick and would we wait a short tome, during which the rain started falling.

After a leisurely coffee, we met up with Hannah again who was feeling better, and all set off. Two of us were well equipped for wet weather, Tim and Lis, one partially, Doris, and one hardly at all, the BBC. The first half was though the city park, marked with the familiar acorn Hadrian's Wall Path signs. We got lost. Too much talking and referring to the wrong page in the guide book saw another about turn.

Once we found a suitably muddy stretch of path and the rain increased Hannah asked for the interview. A not-very-impressed-Doris with the several shortish answers to the BBC's probing questions(?) followed by Tim and then Lis. That was followed by camera shots of us going forwards, backwards and sideways along the path, close-ups of mud, prophetic as it turned out, and sound effects, boots sploshing in mud etc. Much to Doris' disappointment, the BBC session came to a close and after one and a half hours we had covered about three quarters of a mile, worse progress was to come. Hannah left, we set off in grand style, and even the sun came out. We celebrated with a lunch stop beside the sausage works thirty minutes later.

All was going well on a pleasant walk following the River Eden, and we soon reached the village of Grinsdale. We crossed the road and followed the path down to a stile, very elaborately built of steel and wood. After the stile we entered mud... .mud, a sea of mud, heavily pocked cow fields and walkers' boots had turned not just the path but thw whole fields into deep mud and Doris got stuck, Lis helped, Lis got stuck, I helped and we nearly all got stuck. The only answer was to build stepping stone and bridges from rocks we carried from the field edges and broken fencing. Thirty minutes later we had made six hundred yards. And the some more mud, after some steps, and the more. We invented 'fence walking', first using stock fencing, and then a wooden fence. After two hours we had done half a mile and reached a road, to read a notice that this the next section had been closed due to landslip. Lis stayed with Doris while I went to get the car. We covered about four miles in six hours, thanks to the BBC and ... mud.

But it was fun and Doris was as stoic as ever.

Quote of the two days from Doris "I don't get tired." This after Jo had fallen asleep in the car and Tim was nodding off at Gatesgarth.

THE EIGHTH LEG

This amazing creation of nature, a spider taking the shape of a happy face, is as harmless as it seems. It is found in the forests of Hawaii.

Hadrian's Spider Trek VIII

Day 1 Beaumont to Boustead Hill by Doris

Cath, Geoff and I left Ambleside at 8.15 and travelled to Beaumont. We were met by Alison and Norman and two locals who wanted to meet us, due to television. The walk was easy along quiet roads and a bit windy and cold. For our lunch stop, we decided to go a little further to make the next day shorter. The walk was on the side of the shore which was treacherous, kennels and holes etc with grass and marram grass between. Warning signs of depth changes up to four feet, no horses allowed. Television caught up about half way along. The B and B had very large rooms and an enormous bathroom for all six of us. View from window excellent across the inlet to Scotland. It was a sunny afternoon and clear skies at night. Evening meal was at the pub we had visited earlier.

Day 2 Boustead hill to Bowness on Solway by Doris

"Others" gradually arrived, Gwyn, Michael and Beth, Tim and lastly Hugh. It was a lovely sunny day with two more TV representatives at the final finishing point after having reached a playground. After very bad weather forecasts – frost, wind and maybe snow, it was a lovely sunny day. The end was a happy tea provided by our B and B. I was presented with a wonderful hand embroidered picture of the Wall and its surroundings and a fantastic cake to be photographed. We sang songs composed by Norman with many verses.

People drifted off – some home and some to stay overnight.

The end was good.

Day 1 Beaumont to Boustead Hill by Cath

"We just had to come and meet her – we saw her on TV last night!" said two dog walkers on Beaumont Village green. The preparation for this leg centred around mud avoidance. Stick to the road became the mantra for the Hadrian's Wall Path Walkers and high-vis jackets the uniform. Doris was in fine fettle on the way up to the Solway, chattering about people and things that had touched her life during the last few weeks. She set a cracking pace and we reached the Greyhound at Burgh Bay in double quick time.

By then the media phone calls had started: Border TV, BBC Radio Cumbria and the Westmorland Gazette – all wanted a piece of Doris. Andy 1 and Andy 2 from Tyne Tees arrived at the Greyhound and produced a nice news item shown later that day.. Edward I, the Hammer of the Scots, stared wistfully towards Scotland as we rested mid morning. Our resident Scots historian, Norman of the clan McCandlish, told me that Ted II died trying to cross the Solway and conquer Scotland. Why didn't he just pop up the M74?

Onwards Doris marched to the marshy costal Solway plain where most of the traffic seemed to be taking part in the Solway Plain Speed Trials – so much for the high vis jackets. The NTS kept a steady eye on us from his gleaming red Skoda flashing his warning lights to try and slow down the speed merchants.

Lunch in the Boustead Hill Bistro.

Arctic breeze

Doris sharing her lunch with canine friends

silent synchronised slavering dogs.

"Let's carry on" said Doris "It's only half past one."

6.00pm at Hillside Farm and we are poised to watch Border TV or was it ITV – oh well Doris is such an experienced media artist now! On to the Greyhound and a meet up with Rich and Kate from Edinburgh, the advance party of the Arnotts. A volunteer Ranger for the HWP told us the best news yet…our Saturday route is MUD FREE! Yippee we said, then he promptly gave Doris some money for Centre Point. This kept happening in the pub and on the road. And so back to Hillside B and B and bed…….zzzz

THE VERY LAST DAY

Day 2 Beaumont to Bowness on Solway

The great clan gathering started at 9.15 when Tim-up-the-road and Barbara arrived at Bowstead Hill. It was sunny, bright, breezy and cold –perfect walkng weather. The cavalcade of Spider Trekkers made their way to Glasson, once again attracting attention from weekend motorists who stopped to say "Aren't you the lady from the telly?"… then showered Doris with praise and occasionally money; over £144 over the last two days.

Approaching the Highland Laddie, a pub, not Norman, Alison ran ahead to turn on her charm and the owners opened up an hour early especially for us. Mark, the owner, even donated our coffee money, £13.50 back to Doris' Centre Point Fund. We laughed at the amusing mottos on plaques advertising for a Fisherman's Wife and the one about Seagull Management. We decided we would return there in the evening.

Onwards to Port Carlisle via the proper Hadrian's Wall Path at last! It was firm underfoot and a pleasant woodland walk by the sea where the dogs, Alfie, Lucy and Jake could room freely off their leads at last. Lucy and Alfie had a constant battle for possession of THE Stick – a bit like Hadrian and the Scots for the possession of the very land we were walking on. Lunch stop at the children's playground by the Hop and Anchor in Port Carlisle, and out of the west came the second Arnott Battalion who had driven all the way from Essex and St Annes and Leeds to join us for the Last Spider Trek Day.

John, a pleasant young camera man and a reporter from Border TV were waiting as the Spider Trekkers arrived at Banks Promenade where there is a lovely little summer house-cum-gazebo full of poems and interesting things about the Wall, the Solway and various mosaics. Al was thrilled that this last stop was on the site of the Roman fort called Maia, the name of her granddaughter.

The afternoon tea at Wallsend Guest House was delightful. Lyn had put bunting up around the railings and a banner saying

CONGRATULATIONS DORIS

Cliff Richard sang his signature tune and all the guest house guests and Spider Trekkers stood and applauded Doris who stood looking quite bemused and perhaps a little bit embarrassed. A delightfully quirky Hadrian's Wall cake depicting significant moments in the Trek since March was presented to Doris including candles depicting the 84 miles that Doris has walked.

"I can't cut this, it's too good to look at!" she said.

There was a speech of thanks followed by a toast to Doris with sparkling wine. A sing along followed thanks to Norman's ingenuity with words accompanied by Cath on the piano, and then Doris gave lovely presents of books to all her fellow trekkers. Although this is the end of the Journal, Doris' work will continue. Nothing is surer than that.

THE END